Protest Song

Tim Price is a former journalist from the South Wales valleys. As well as writing for stage and television, he hosts a new writing night in a Mongolian yurt in Cardiff called Dirty Protest. Tim was one of eight candidates to be selected for the BBC Drama Writers' Academy 2009 and was awarded a bursary by the BBC and Royal Court in 2006 as one of 'The 50' best emerging writers in the UK. His plays include *For Once* (Pentabus Theatre), *Salt, Root and Roe* (Donmar Warehouse/Trafalgar Studios), *The Radicalisation of Bradley Manning* (National Theatre Wales and winner of the James Tait Black Drama Prize) and *I'm With the Band* (Traverse Theatre).

Tim Price

Protest Song

B L O O M S B U R Y

LONDON · NEW DELHI · NEW YORK · SYDNEY

Bloomsbury Methuen Drama
An imprint of Bloomsbury Publishing Plc

50 Bedford Square	1385 Broadway
London	New York
WC1B 3DP	NY 10018
UK	USA

www.bloomsbury.com

Bloomsbury is a registered trade mark of Bloomsbury Publishing Plc

First published 2014
Reprinted 2014

© Tim Price 2014

Tim Price has asserted his right under the Copyright, Designs
and Patents Act, 1988, to be identified as author of this work.

This version of the text went to print before the end of rehearsals
and may differ slightly from the version performed.

All rights whatsoever in this play are strictly reserved and application
for performance, etc. should be made before rehearsals begin to
Independent Talent Group Limited, Oxford House, 76 Oxford Street,
London W1D 1BS. No performance may be given unless a licence
has been obtained.

No rights in incidental music or songs contained in the work are hereby
granted and performance rights for any performance/presentation
whatsoever must be obtained from the respective copyright owners.

British Library Cataloguing-in-Publication Data
A catalogue record for this book is available from the British Library.

ISBN: PB: 978-1-4725-7705-4
ePUB: 978-1-4725-7707-8
ePDF: 978-1-4725-7706-1

Library of Congress Cataloging-in-Publication Data
A catalog record for this book is available from the Library of Congress.

Typeset by Country Setting, Kingsdown, Kent CT14 8ES
Printed and bound in Great Britain

in memory of
Antonia Bird

Introduction

> 'Hemp-smoking, fornicating hippies,
> in crusty little tents'.
>
> *Boris Johnson – Mayor of London,*
> *at a £500-a-head masked ball,*
> *for the banking sector in 2011*

There's a restaurant in Borough that overlooks the market, called Roast. High up and glass panelled, it specializes in roasting all kinds of meats. It has many selling points, but for me it will forever be the restaurant in which I burst into tears because I couldn't write a play.

That play was *Protest Song*, and I was a week away from starting rehearsals. This was not an isolated incident. There was also the screaming down the phone episode on the M57, and the ugly childcare stand-off on the half-landing.

This play has not wanted to come out. This usually happens when you know the story. When you can talk about the story. When everyone you tell says 'that's a really good story'. When the National Theatre of Great Britain and Northern Ireland says 'that's such a good story, we'll produce it'. When others share your conviction, this is when plays come over all coy. The other plays, the ones that no one wants, have no such self-esteem issues. If there were a Premier League for writing plays that no one wants, I would be the Ryan Giggs of playwrights. People would marvel at my longevity, my relentless appetite for rejection, and write colour pieces on my first rejection, the one that set me off on that magnificent run. I am far more successful at not writing a play for Polly Findlay and Rhys Ifans at the National than I am at writing one.

When we first approached Rhys with the play, the first thing he said was 'I'm not interested in doing a play about homelessness at the National Theatre, where everyone feels safe.' We talked for a long time about a feeling we could all relate to, of being on the same tube as someone who doesn't know the rules. The play I had written was a safe play about homelessness. Danny told the audience his story, moving as it was, but he obeyed all the rules and conventions we have grown accustomed to. You could watch the first draft of *Protest Song*, leave the theatre and roll along the South Bank in your hamster ball of comfort, unblemished from the evening's theatrical assault.

If we could tell Danny's story through the prism of tube-carriage terror then there was a chance Danny's story would be felt, rather than understood. This took the drama from Danny's story-telling and placed it firmly in the relationship between Danny and the audience. All of us agreed the drama needed to be live, rather than recalled.

So started my epic odyssey of tears, tantrums and redrafts as I tried and failed to re-render our story into the moment. I have a document on my laptop called '*Protest Song* cut stuff'. It is three times the length of the final play.

Rehearsals started on November 18th, and hearing it read every day sent me running home to rewrite again and again. I wrote three drafts in the first three days, but still it didn't work, Rhys said he felt like a 'shell in a tsunami of words'. I told him to go fuck himself. Or maybe that was something I wrote and then cut, I can't remember, it was a busy time. Either way, I was still failing to get the story in the room, and then, God bless the stage managers at the National, halfway through week one we were told that we could use the Shed to rehearse.

My whole problem with the play, since we decided to reimagine the play was that I couldn't reimagine the play. I couldn't let go of the old Danny. The Danny who would say what he felt. The Danny who could make connections between things that happened to him. I couldn't let go of the

part of Danny that was me. But when I saw Rhys on the stage
in the Shed, surrounded by all the empty seats, I finally saw
the Danny we all wanted to make. It all fell into place. The
potential for Danny to strike a rapport with one member of
the audience and to take a dislike to another. The chance for
Danny to confront or commune with a group of people. The
slowest, stickiest penny I have ever swallowed finally dropped
and all I had to do now was shit it out and give it to Rhys Ifans.

By the end of week one I had written six complete rewrites.
Everyone, everywhere told me to stop writing, but I couldn't,
because now I could see the play, I wanted to make up for lost
time, I needed to get this right.

Because, this play is desperately important to me. Not just
because of where it is, or whom I'm making it with, but
because of whom it is about. In 2008, then a candidate in
the mayoral race, Boris Johnson said he would eradicate
homelessness in London by 2012. By now, under Johnson's
mayorship, homelessness has doubled. In 2013, when Johnson
compared the suffering felt by those castigated for their
wealth to the homeless of London, his abject and total failure
regarding homelessness in London made sense.

Occupy is a platform, not an operating system. It is not
designed to tell us what to think or how to be. It is designed
for us to discover ourselves. And for the millions upon millions
of us who did not take up that invitation, Occupy remains a
confusing episode we privately resent for not packaging and
commodifying their message into an easily tweetable slogan.
But for the few thousand who did take up the invitation, the
repercussions of participating will last longer than any party
manifesto, or election promise. It is this story I felt compelled to
tell.

Tim Price,
December 2013

Acknowledgements

To Ben Power and all at the National Theatre, Polly Findlay, Rhys Ifans, Sean Linnen, Merle Hensel, Nicky Lund, Cathy King, Anna Brewer, Mark Jefferies, Gary Marsh, Menna Price, Phil Price, Franklin Moss Price, Matthew Price, Maryline Price, Joseph Price and Sophia Price, those at Crisis, Shelter, The Basement and Broadway London, who have helped with research, and all rough-sleepers, Occupiers, and Jim Mcmahon who have inspired me with their stories. Thanks especially to Chloë Moss for saving this play.

Protest Song

Can anyone make a difference any more?
Can anyone write a protest song?

'Let Robeson Sing'
Manic Street Preachers

National Theatre

The National Theatre, where *Protest Song* had its premiere in December 2013, is central to the creative life of the UK. In its three theatres on the South Bank in London it presents an eclectic mix of new plays and classics from the world repertoire, with seven or eight productions in repertory at any one time. And through an extensive programme of amplifying activities – Platform Performances, backstage tours, foyer music, publications, exhibitions and outdoor events – it recognises that theatre doesn't begin and end with the rise and fall of the curtain. The National endeavours to maintain and re-energise the great traditions of the British stage and to expand the horizons of audiences and artists alike. It aspires to reflect in its repertoire the diversity of the nation's culture. It takes a particular responsibility for the creation of new work – offering at the NT Studio a space for research and development for the NT's stages and the theatre as a whole. Through its Learning programme, it invites people of all ages to discover the NT's repertoire, the skills and excitement of theatre-making, and the building itself. As the national theatre, it aims to foster the health of the wider British theatre through policies of collaboration and touring. These activities demonstrate the considerable public benefit provided by the NT, both locally and nationally. Between 20 and 26 new productions are staged each year in one of the NT's three theatres. Last year, the National's total reach was 3.6 million people worldwide, through attendances on the South Bank, in the West End, on tour and through National Theatre Live, the digital broadcast of live performances to cinema screens all over the world.

Information: +44(0) 20 7452 3400
Box Office: +44(0) 20 7452 3000
National Theatre, South Bank, London SE1 9PX
www.nationaltheatre.org.uk
Registered Charity No: 224223

Protest Song was first performed in The Shed at the National Theatre on 16 December 2013.

Danny   Rhys Ifans

Director   Polly Findlay
Designer   Merle Hensel
Lighting Designer   Lee Curran
Movement Director – Jack Murphy
Sound Designer   Carolyn Downing
Voice and Dialect Coach   Richard Ryder
Staff Director   Sean Linnen

Characters

Danny, *forty-something, homeless alcoholic from the South Wales valleys*

Notes

The performer and director should feel free to create bespoke interaction with the audience and space.

Jenny's second phone call is not intended to be heard by the audience.

A dash (−) indicates an interruption of word or thought.

Words or phrases in brackets (. . .) are unfinished thoughts or sentences and where possible should remain unspoken. This is to be discovered in rehearsal at the director and performer's discretion.

A forward slash (/) indicates when the following line should overlap.

One

In the space, **Danny** *sits in audience members' seats until he is moved along. This continues until there is nowhere left for him to sit.*

Improvise his transgressions with audience members.

He makes it down to the stage.

Danny (*to patron*)   Ow, have you got a pound for a hostel?

He looms.

Patron gets purse out and gives him a pound.

Danny   Thank you, thank you.

He realises he can make more.

It's three-twenty actually for a hostel. Have you got three-twenty?

Patron gets purse out.

Danny   Come on, you're minted.

Patron gives him the money.

Danny   Happy Christmas.

Beat.

A mobile phone starts ringing from **Danny***'s bag. A moment before he realises it's his phone.*

He scrambles to opens his rucksack. He pulls out a plastic bag tied with rubber bands. Desperately he pulls the rubber bands off and pulls off the bag, to reveal another. This goes on for some time as he unties layer after layer of plastic bags, the phone ringing all the while. Finally he gets to the phone.

Danny: Yes!

But his celebrations are cut short when the phone stops ringing.

Fuck.

The phone beeps with a text message.

Voicemail (*on answer phone*)   You have one new message. To listen to your messages, press one.

Danny *presses the button.*

Jenny (*voice only*)   Danny it's Jenny, I'm at Waterloo Bridge, got the paperwork, bit of a scramble but I've got it. Just need you to sign now. So. Hurry up! I'm a bit pushed for time. Give me a call yeah, let me know you're on your way.

As **Danny** *listens he winces, realising he'd forgotten. He scrambles and starts packing his all his property back into his bag.*

Danny   Housing charity give me this, just got to look after this, keep it charged, and I'll get indoors by Christmas, my own bed, central heating, the fucking works. I done all the pathway shit, counselling, life-skills, detox.

He packs some cans of lager.

I know what I'm doing – when I was indoors, I was the one who sorted everything out, knew where everything was.

In his haste, he forgets to pack the phone.

I fucking like order, not in an OCD way but y'know . . . 'Where's my kit, Dad?' 'Where's my bag?' And they wanna test my fucking reliability. Fucking mugs.

He swaggers off.

Then realises he hasn't got the phone and runs back.

Fucking hell!

Holds phone.

Nearly failed the fucking test, fucking first day. Oh you fucking cock-head.

Beat.

Last time I did the pathway I didn't even get to the phone test and Occupy came along and fucked it up. The Square Mile's perfect for rough sleepers 'cause it's dead at night. Non-residential, seven years I've been there, it's quiet.

Beat.

Quiet until three thousand people turn up on your doorstep with tents and bongos.

Two

'OI! FUCK OFF! THIS IS A FUCKING CATHEDRAL.'

I'm a free spirit, don't get me wrong. I think people should do what they want.

'FUCK OFF! TAKE YOUR DRUMS, AND STICK THEM UP YOUR ARSE OR I'M GOING TO FUCKING STAB YOU. FUCK (OFF). THIS IS MY HOME.'

Do what you want, just don't fuck with my routine. It's all I've got.

'Desperate? I'm fucking desperate for you lot to fuck off. How can I sleep? Go on. fuck off.'

Fucking five hundred tents on my doorstep. It was the noise that got to me you know. I think anyone would have done what I did. Any right thinking member of society.

Beat.

So, I piss on a few tents. Early hours, take a stroll. Piss on a few. Pull a few poles out. Slash a couple, 'cause it *will* happen if you – (rough sleep in a tent). If sleeping in a tent was safe, we'd all be doing it? No. You're a target, you mugs. Piss, fire – (the works). So I'm doing them a favour. Better to have *my* piss than a junky's.

Beat.

But what do the cunts do?

Beat.

Build a fucking wigwam. 'Fucking take it down. Fucking take it down now. You are not. This is – (my home). Look at the police here. Look at them. You're fucking trespassing.' Fruit. They used to hand out. *Avocados*, which are actually quite nice. 'Stick this fucking pear up your arse until it comes out of your big toe.' Cunts bring me a poem instead. 'I've got a poem,' I say, and I recite *The Snail and the Whale*. All by heart.

He drinks.

My boy's favourite, that.

He drinks.

(*To patron.*) What's your number. love? What's your number?

Beat.

WHAT'S YOUR FUCKING NUMBER? Sorry. Sorry.

Patron replies with number. **Danny** *announces it as he types it into his phone.*

Danny   It's just I need to look like I'm using it. If I feel *ownership* over it then I won't forget it, in *her* book, *this*:

Phone.

Is civilisation. So let's show her how fucking civilised I am. What's your fucking name love?

Patron replies. **Danny** *puts it in.*

Danny (*to another patron*)   Oi. What's your fucking number?

Patron 2 replies.

Danny   Pass it round. Put all your numbers in, I'm not having anything fuck this up, this time.

Beat.

It wasn't *just* Occupy's fault. St Paul's played a fucking part an' all. They were like, 'Occupy, come and stay!' And then they fucking closed the doors, not just to them but to everyone. Fucking Jesus didn't close his doors to any cunt. Seven years I *slept* outside that door. Wash in there every morning. If I don't wash on the street, I get ill, I get fucking infections, end up in hospital, they know, I told them that.

'I'm nothing to do with those cunts, you know that, Lesley. OPEN THE FUCKING DOOR.' I reckon it was fucking

Boris, he made them close. He fucking put us in detention centres for the Olympics; didn't fucking know that, did you? He's a fucking shit-eating Nazi paedophile. He's the one who's behind the benches with dividers, sloping bus seats, one bag at a time in libraries. Bleach! He makes them pour fucking bleach on doorways.

Beat.

Meant to be a fucking refuge and a couple of tents – (close it down). The Blitz couldn't close that church. I was in the middle, Occupy don't want to listen, St Paul's don't want to listen. 'OPEN THIS FUCKING' DOOR NOW.' I can't remember how it happened, but Allie the fruit girl turns up, and hears what's going on. 'MIC CHECK! MIC CHECK!' she shouts.

Beat.

And I shit you not; the whole fucking camp shouts it back. The human microphone they call it.

Beat.

'THE CHURCH HAS CLOSED ITS DOORS. THEY WON'T LET DANNY IN. THEY RECKON IT'S CLOSED UNTIL THE CAMP IS EVICTED', or something like that, and they all fucking shout it back. Together. And suddenly. The *whole* fucking camp is listening, every *single* one of them.

Beat.

How fucking handy would that be when you're getting stabbed or pissed on, or you can't find your . . .

He panics, can't find his phone.

Where's my phone? Who's got my phone.

He retrieves it.

He chooses a patron, hands them the phone.

You. Keep an eye.

Beat.

After that, I'm like a fucking celebrity, 'Do you want a cup of tea?' 'Do you want a tent?' 'Do you want to join the church liaison working group?' 'Come and join this group, come and meet this little bloke, sign that.' I fucking preferred it when they were ignoring me.

Beat.

They were like ants. Two days they had a fucking kitchen. With a chef. He had a hat!

Beat.

Allie took me in, food spread out. Just help yourself. Different kinds of bread, tea, coffee, soup, cheese. One meat dish, one veg dish. Queues of people, in the middle of fucking St Paul's. They'd only been there two days. Worse than the fucking gypos. There's no ticketing, just in and out. I'm in there with my can, no cunt says anything. Allie's like, 'Have whatever you want.' FUCK OFF. I don't want anything do with this shit. 'It's free.'

He double-takes.

Free food. On my doorstep.

He considers this.

Well.

Beat.

Be rude not to, wouldn't it?

Beat.

Odd bowl of soup.

Beat.

Breakfast, maybe dinner, see what's on for tea. No one says anything.

Beat.

Not long before I'm fucking rinsing them.

Beat.

Eat like a fucking oligarch. Every day. No one says anything.

Beat.

I put my bowl in the bucket. They have this big square bucket. And I remember, when I was indoors a bit of hoovering never bothered me; ironing, did it all, long as you got a bit of music it's fine, but I fucking *hated* washing up. I'd cook just to avoid it. I'd do anything to avoid it, harder when you're not working. The wife would say, 'You don't wash up 'cause you're a bum.'

He looks at the imaginary bowl.

And there's this bucket.

Beat.

And I've got the bowl, and I don't know why but I put my hands in under the water.

(*To himself.*) Drown the cow out.

Beat.

Fucking squirt some washing-up liquid, rub it, swill it round, rinse it off –

He startles.

'Fuck me.'

He holds an imaginary bowl for inspection.

'I just cleaned a bowl.'

Beat.

Wooky, this guy with dreadlocks, takes it off me, dries it and stacks it on the shelves. 'Shall we crack on?' He wants me to carry on washing up. Thinks I'm a fucking volunteer, thinks I'm gonna wash up after all these cunts, no chance.

He is confused.

But I fill up the bucket and I fucking do it.

Beat.

I was down Covent Garden, making a bit of money.

Beat.

Get my spot under a cashpoint. Put my hat out.

Beat.

And start my routine. In the mornings, I have to look exhausted and stay quiet, because that's how *you* feel in the mornings. So I get my face on.

He makes a sad, tired face.

And I make a bit of money.

He pulls the face again.

But for some reason I sort of feel, stupid. I try and ignore it and concentrate, take it serious.

He pulls his sad, tired face.

I don't know what the fuck is the matter with me. It never bothers me normally. I know the fucking game. Mornings I have to look sad and tired and not speak to you. Afternoons I have to do something productive like sell the *Big Issue* or do a drawing on the pavement, and evenings I have to act like I'm desperate to get home to a hostel. Because that's what *you* feel like in the day. Knackered, productive and homesick and it's a way of *acting* like we're connected or something. Like we're the same, I've got it fucking *nailed*.

Beat.

Rinsed it for years.

Beat.

But now, I feel stupid. With my hat on the floor.

Beat.

I sort of get to know them while I'm doing the washing up. Wooky's got an Anonymous mask and I ask him what it's all about.

'It's Guy Fawkes. It's from a comic book', and he goes on about Anonymous, so I try and steer him away from politics, I am not interested in that shit. 'Guy Fawkes, makes me think of my boy. Every bonfire night we'd go out, and he'd always check the bonfires for hedgehogs. Whenever I see a firework and it looks like a hedgehog, I sort of hope he can see it as well', that sort of thing, just making conversation.

Beat.

Wooky's like an angry uncle, gets stressed about the smallest things, like people not bringing cutlery back, Allie is like the mum, like a diplomat making sure everyone's being kind to each other. She sort of makes the kitchen really welcoming 'cause she treats everyone like a long-lost friend. Hal is the Buddhist who normally lives in communes so he's really quiet; he's like Grandad in the corner, wise and bald. And then Dad is Dev, he's the chef, he runs everything but he's the most awkward man on the planet, you'd never go to him with anything.

Beat.

Wooky's doing impressions of everyone – he does a brilliant Hal, he's got his fucking, the way he talks just right and then Dev he's got his walk down to a 't', it's sort like –

He does an impression but gives up half-way through.

He must just watch everyone all day, he does Allie's greeting and everyone pisses themselves laughing it's spot-on, even Allie's fucking laughing, she can see what she's like.

He is itching to join in.

'I've got one!' I say.

He shifts his weight uncomfortably.

Pause.

Only. I haven't.

Beat.

And they're all looking at me.

Beat.

And I don't know why, but I just. Carry on washing up.

He is embarrassed.

Beat.

Sometimes an old woman in a poncho comes in to wash up, and when she does I go and stand by the shelves.

He is embarrassed.

Pass them stuff. I sort of invent a new role. Like a, like a shelf-sweeper. My first Saturday on the shelves was a bit stressful, lunchtime; there was queue all the way past the tech tent. Wooky and Allie serving, Dev and Hal cooking and Poncho, or Carol as she likes to be called, is on the sink and me on the shelves. 'Danny, get us the lentils', 'Danny, cutlery', 'Danny, where's the fucking bread?' 'FUCKING SLOW IT UP.'

He is sheepish.

So when it calms down, I think perhaps I'd better head off, they probably don't want me around, but before I go I give the shelves a bit of a tidy. Bring a bit of *order*.

There's no system, they've got no system. it's just shoved there, so I separate them all out, get all the perishables together, all the crockery, and all the tins. Dried goods. Get a bit of fucking order in there. It only takes me half hour and it's all sorted, easy to navigate, for the next fucking mug who's roped in.

Beat.

Couple of days later I'm in the queue and Poncho's on the shelves.

He can barely hide his irritation.

'Can I have the soup please, Carol?'

His irritation rises.

'Soup please, Carol?'

He can barely stand still.

'Carol?'

'IT'S FUCKING THERE, CAROL. TOP RIGHT. WITH ALL THE OTHER FUCKING TINS. IN THE TIN SECTION.'

He straightens himself.

I don't know why it pisses me off so much. It's just a shelving system. But it's so simple, why is she making a fucking meal of it, the fat little Mexican? I spent hours on that. The longer I watch, the more I want to fucking smash her face in.

'Kidney beans, Carol?'

He is aggravated.

'Carol?'

'Out the way poncho, I can't take any more of this. Right, who needs what?' And I get in front of the shelves, and I don't even think, I just fucking rinse it. Chickpeas are flying here, sweet potatoes flying there. All afternoon, everyone gets what they want. And I fucking prove that my system, my system of dividing it all up, means you know where everything is without thinking, it's just there. And I don't shout or swear or frighten anyone. Job done. Proved my point.

'Nice to see your face again, Danny,' says Dev. 'Nice to have you back.'

He is confused.

Between the washing up, and the shelves and the prep, there's always something to do, something needs doing. So when the journalist comes in I just carry on chopping carrots. She asks them all why we're here.

Hal goes first, he says something like: 'Spiritual bankruptcy.'

Wooky says, 'I want a revolution.' Allie goes on about loads of stuff I don't understand and Dev says, 'I'm not sure why I'm here, I just read about it, thought it was important.'

'And you? Why are you here?'

'I'm doing the carrots.'

'Why are you protesting?'

'Oh, I'm not part of the protest, I'm just helping out.'

Beat.

'Why are you helping out?'

'I don't know.'

'Why are you helping in the *kitchen*?'

'I don't know. It just sort of happened.'

'You must have a reason.'

And she's looking at me, and I'm thinking I want to know as well, I don't know why I keep coming in I'm spending all my fucking time in here, I don't know why, it doesn't make any sense.

'I'm lonely,' I say.

He is ashamed.

He smiles.

I like the routine. Half-six the cleaners wake me up on the steps. I know Dev's opening up on his own, so I head down there, get the water. Start poaching eggs for him. Bit of banter.

Beat.

When it's not busy, and we've done our prep, if it's just me and Dev, he teaches me how to cook. I learn how to cook –

okra, mung beans, pak choy, all sorts of mad shit I'd never buy. It was brilliant, two blokes in a massive kitchen. Just sautéing all kinds of mad shit for each other. And the routine helps. If I've got a routine I don't get into trouble up here.

He taps his head.

It's great because he doesn't want to get involved or stick his nose in, not like Allie or Jenny, he doesn't want to know any of that shit. He's so awkward. He's perfect company if you want to keep things to yourself. But sometimes, you can't help it.

Beat.

We were in the kitchen, just the two of us, doing an audit for the day, and Dev reads out a, a sell-by date and I realise it's Kylie's birthday. I get a bit upset. I'm crying, and Dev goes:

'Do you wanna mint?'

He laughs.

It's just like being back in prison, there's all sorts there. Mentally ill, professors, drug dealers, soldiers, bankers, musicians. And every one of them is fucking Allie's mate. She introduces me to everyone as 'Danny from-the-kitchen,' and it sort of becomes my new name. 'Danny from-the-kitchen'. Even now, sometimes when I meet someone I'm like 'I'm Danny f –

Beat.

There's this knackered piano outside the kitchen tent, out of tune, keys missing. Every cunt plays it all the time. Fucking chopsticks or 'The Entertainer', it is torture.

Beat.

But this bloke comes along, and he spends hours pressing all the keys, over and over again. Like he was testing it, or getting to know it.

Beat.

And after a while, he starts to figure it out. He doesn't fix all the broken bits, he just learns where they are and plays around it.

Beat.

We've been fantasising about all the different ways we could destroy this fucking piano for weeks, and then this bloke comes along and it's fucking beautiful. He just knew what it needed to make music again.

Beat.

Allie is so excited, she wants to dance, but Dev is too uptight, Wooky says it's too bourgeois and Hal's a Buddhist. I don't know why they don't dance but they don't, and she looks at me, and I think I'm not getting involved in any of this.

'I'll dance with you,' I say and she nearly vaults the table.

He looks down at himself and is repulsed.

He holds his hands out at a distance.

He realises his hands are dirty and he furiously rubs his hands clean.

He holds his hands out at a distance.

He dances as if holding Allie.

'Hold me properly,' she says, and she pulls me close. People don't touch me. I'm not . . . I'm not used to it. I never bump into anyone or brush past anyone. 'Cause people go.

He recoils.

She's holding me and I'm confused, people don't touch rough-sleepers do they?

He addresses a patron.

Danny   Would you touch a rough-sleeper?

He addresses patrons until someone says 'yes'.

When someone says yes, **Danny***'s heart melts.*

Danny   You would.

Summoning courage, he offers his hand to the patron.

Danny   Would you?

Beat.

Please?

*He persists until patron joins **Danny** on stage.*

As he takes her in his arms we hear piano music. They dance, and slowly, **Danny** *turns patron so he is facing the audience and she is facing the back of the set.*

*We see **Danny** is overcome with happiness.*

Danny   We dance.

Beat.

We dance around the kitchen, and she puts her head on my chest.

Danny *and patron dance.*

Danny   We dance, and it's just me and her and I don't feel disgusting or repulsive anymore.

He is in agony.

And I hold on to him and I promise I'll never let go.

He holds the patron as if it is the last time he held his son.

And then slowly he comes to.

Improvise. Perhaps he is embarrassed and apologises as he lets go of her.

Thank you.

Patron returns to her seat.

Danny *gathers himself and drinks heavily from his can.*

Beat.

Danny   I tell her my ex-wife said I'll die alone, because I'm the most selfish man she's ever met. We sit on Banksy's Monopoly board together, and she tells me Allie isn't her real name. Her real name's Lucy. 'Allie's my activist name. She's who I want to be: changing the world. Lucy's a victim.' And we get pissed and watch bankers kick tents, and tourists take pictures, London go by, and for some reason it all feels new.

Beat.

The more people I meet, the more I start to understand what's going on, like, I met a blind diabetic woman in a wheelchair, with kidney and heart problems and the Government declared her fit to work. She was fucking double incontinent.

Beat.

Met a shop owner. He'd borrow money off the bank every month to buy stock, sell the clothes and then pay off the loan. The bank just fucking stopped lending to him. Just like that. He went bust overnight with a wife and kids.

Beat.

Every day there was someone. I was in the Info tent and this bloke comes in, he's in a super expensive suit, but looks like shit. Looks like he could do with a good meal, or a good sleep, I don't know what, but he needs something. He wants to make a donation. He gets his wallet out and gives us everything he's got and he starts to cry.

He's a millionaire, he's got wife, kids, mistresses, but he's the most unhappy bloke I've ever met and *I* end up comforting *him.* That's the kind of mad shit that would happen in Occupy.

Beat.

Three

Danny But I was still avoiding the politics. All this shit.

Up-twinkles. Down-twinkles. **Danny** *gives them the 'V'.*

I didn't get involved in all that.

Allie comes in, 'Come on, you're coming to the GA tonight.'

'Thank you, no, I've got plans tonight.' I haven't got plans, but with Allie you've got to be on your toes, or you'll be roped into some nonsense.

'Please. It's a big one.'

'No, I've got plans, and besides I'm not a protestor.'

And she looks me dead in the eyes.

'It would make me happy.'

He doesn't know what to do with the attention.

It goes on for ages.

He clears his throat.

The way a General Assembly works is, they're held twice a day on the steps of St Paul's at twelve-thirty, and seven o'clock. The Assembly listens to proposals, and then votes on them. If there's consensus then the proposal is passed.

He gets some chalks.

The proposals come from working groups.

He grabs some chalk and draws on the tiles small groups.

And they meet every week.

He draws a bigger group.

The proposals go to Process and the Process junkies then –

He draws a bigger group.

– feed them in to the General Assembly. And you vote like this:

Up-twinkles.

Everyone.

Everyone joins in.

That means you agree.

Down-twinkles.

Disagree.

Um . . .

'*C*'.

Clarification. And there's a couple of others but the big one is this.

Crosses arms.

A block. If one person blocks, the motion can't pass. Only needs one. It can pass if you –

Down-twinkles.

But if you –

Block.

– it all falls apart. I saw fights break out over blocks. Anonymous were the fucking masters of blocking.

Beat.

Wooky, Hal and Dev are there already, so all the kitchen crew sit together. It goes on for an hour or so, and there's proposals about sanitation, and the church, and what we should do about the banks.

'Join in,' says Allie, 'cause she can see that I haven't voted once.

'Do you agree with anything that's been said?'

'I don't know.'

'You must have an opinion.'

Beat.

'It doesn't matter what I think.'

And as I say that, Dev goes, 'Shh shh.' It's the city liaison group, and the whole GA goes quiet for the first time, like everyone's been waiting for this proposal. This little mousey girl gets up to the mic with a piece of paper.

'The City of London has agreed not to pursue any legal actions, or attempts to evict us, on condition we agree to leave peacefully and clean up after ourselves on December 31st. How do we respond?'

(*Impersonation.*) 'I think we should accept the offer; we've made our point.' (*Impersonation.*) 'If we accept this we can leave in a non-violent manner.' (*Impersonation.*) 'Our priority is a non-violent eviction.' (*Impersonation.*) 'If we accept we can ask for a permanent, symbolic tent on site.'

'NO! NO! NO! NO! NO! NO! NO. WHAT THE FUCK IS WRONG WITH YOU? LET'S NOT ACCEPT THE OFFER. LET'S NOT ASK FOR A FUCKING SYMBOLIC TENT. YOU THINK THIS IS SYMBOLIC? WHAT THE FUCK DO I SYMBOLISE? WHAT ABOUT ALL THE ROUGH-SLEEPERS? WHERE ARE WE GONNA GO? THIS IS A PROTEST. NOT A CAMP SITE.'

He catches his breath.

He looks around.

And, everywhere, I look, I see –

Up-twinkles.

So I do it back. 'You don't do it back, it's just our way of agreeing with you,' says Allie.

Beat.

It's just our way of agreeing. With my point. Which I made.
In public. I made a point. In public. In front of. Hundreds, of
people. In public.

He giggles at the insanity.

And the facilitator goes, 'I think we have consensus', and they
fucking jump on me! Hal, Wooky, Allie, none of them have
got consensus before. And we roll around on the steps and
Dev takes pictures on his phone because he doesn't like being
touched and Wooky gets up and does an impression of me.
And they all do it and they all take the piss out of me.

He loves it.

For me now the camp and the politics were interconnected.
The camp couldn't exist without the politics, and the politics
couldn't exist without the camp. You can't have one without
the other. I hadn't realised, I was too caught up in my own
shit.

He points to his head.

But that GA changed everything, 'cause, when you see five
hundred people going –

Up-twinkles.

There was no going back.

The big picture that they don't want you to see is that
everything is connected.

Because I used to think I'm just an alki. But I'm not. I'm loads
of things.

He puts a can down. Points to it.

That's not gonna fix everything. What about the fact I'm a
dad? And a metal-presser. A man. A fucking full-back. A
divorcee. A rough-sleeper. A chef. A *ninety-nine percenter*? What
about all that? I'm not just an alki, and it's not just a banking
crisis.

Beat.

Those poor cunts under the bridge who you walked past. They're connected to you.

Beat.

I'd go in the tea tent and I'd sit with a paranoid schizophrenic, a banker, a runaway, a professor and a tranny, and we'd all have something in common. Getting fucked by the one per cent. I wouldn't have done that before Occupy. But now the picture was bigger. I was finally in it. Connected, affecting others.

Beat.

I don't just want to see my son again, I want to abolish tuition fees, I want civil rights in Egypt, I want to stop drilling in the Arctic, I want all of that stuff! I start going on marches. I go on every march I can. On the electricians' union one I get fucking kettled. Kettling to me was having boiling water with sugar thrown over your face, but on the streets it's about stopping you moving. Me kettled! Anyone see the fucking irony in that? Seven years those mugs have been moving me on. Now I've got to stay put! So they can set their dogs on sparks who just want to protect their jobs.

'BALFOUR BEATTY SHAME ON YOU!'

'BALFOUR BEATTY SHAME ON YOU!'

Eight hours on Blackfriars Bridge and it's fucking brilliant because we're all together fucking changing the world.

'BALFOUR BEATTY SHAME ON YOU!'

He looks at the crowd. A surge of passion.

MIC CHECK.

Audience responds.

(*Louder.*) MIC CHECK!

Audience responds.

(*Louder.*) MIC CHECK!

Audience responds.

BORIS JOHNSON –

Audience responds.

IS A MASSIVE CUNT.

Audience responds.

THE EVENING STANDARD –

Audience responds.

ARE A BUNCH OF CUNTS.

Audience responds.

THE METROPOLITAN POLICE –

Audience responds.

ARE A PACK OF CUNTS.

Audience responds.

Let's sing a fucking carol!

He might write the words up on the tiles, improvising as he moves amongst the audience, instructing certain sections to sing certain lines.

'On the first day of Christmas the system gave to me.
A vote in a democracy.' Got that *right*?

On the second day it's 'Two racist cops'.

On the third day it's 'Three student loans'.

Fourth day – 'Four bailed-out banks'.

Fifth day – 'Boris is a cunt'.

Sixth day – 'Six hacks a-hacking'.

Seventh day – 'Seven drones a-bombing'.

Eighth day – 'Eight sweatshops sweating'.

Ninth day – 'Nine spies surveilling'.

Tenth day – 'Ten MPs claiming'.

Eleventh day – 'Eleven bubbles bursting'.

Twelfth day – 'Twelve councils cutting'.

Once the twelfth day has been sung –

Mobile phone rings. The person holding **Danny***'s phone runs to him. When he sees who's ringing his face falls. He indicates for the audience to stop singing.*

Danny (*improvise*)   Fuck! Shh shh! Everyone! Shh! Oh shit . . . shh, fuck. Shit. Fuck. Bollocks. Everyone . . . shh . . .

He takes the phone. **Jenny***'s lines are unheard.*

Danny   Hello?

Jenny   Danny, it's Jenny.

Danny   Yes. Hi.

Jenny   Where the hell are you?

Danny   I'm, with some, with some friends.

Jenny   Drinking?

Danny   No. Carol singing.

Jenny   Carol *singing*.

Danny   I am.

Jenny   What about the HCTB1 form? I've got it here for you to sign?

Danny   Oh! Was that tonight? Shit.

Jenny   Yes, it was tonight! We arranged this morning when I gave you the phone.

Danny   Where are you now?

Jenny   I'm on a train to Kent.

Danny   I don't understand. Will I be in for Christmas?

Jenny   No. It's too late.

Danny *is gutted.*

Jenny   I had people in the office waiting for it. I've got people in Croydon waiting to process it because I rang them up and told them your story and they're using their own time, to get you in for Christmas and you can't be bothered to turn up.

Danny   Don't cry, Jenny.

Beat.

Come on. Look. Come on.

Jenny   I thought we were getting somewhere.

Danny   We are.

Jenny   I'm doing everything I can to help you.

Danny   I know you are.

Jenny   I'm doing everything.

Danny   I know you are.

Jenny   I thought we were getting somewhere.

Danny   I know, I'm sorry.

Jenny   I've had to ring everyone and *apologise.*

Danny   I'm sorry I just got, distracted. Stop crying, go home, see your family. Don't worry about me. I'll be fine. I'll be fine.

Jenny   I'm just so disappointed.

Danny   I know. Sorry Jenny. Sorry. Sorry. I'm sorry. I'm sorry. I'm sorry. Merry Christmas.

He hangs up.

Four

Danny *looks at his phone.*

The weight of the phone call hits him.

Defeated, he sits down and lights a cigarette.

Danny Anyone done a Crisis at Christmas? (*Dry.*) They're great.

Beat.

No, you know. Good people, volunteering on Christmas Day, fair play.

Beat.

Can't drink though, so everyone wolfs their food down.

Beat.

You're not really celebrating Christmas though. Sitting around with a load of rough-sleepers and people with nowhere else to go. You're sort of getting together to mourn Christmas. To mourn Christmas, and all the Christmases you've fucked up for other people.

He toasts the sentiment.

To Christmas.

A nihilistic smile breaks across his face before he takes a hefty, medicating swig of lager.

Christmas at Occupy was good, that was the best one since – It was great, everyone who'd moved off came back for a day. Say goodbye.

Beat.

And then one night, I was doing a shift in the kitchen, and loads of my old rough-sleeping mates come in because Occupy had closed down the tea tent. The tea tent was the only twenty-four-hour tent, the only place you could stay warm if you didn't have a tent. It was like the Occupy pub for rough-sleepers. But the GA had enough of the noise and shut it down. So the brew-crew all start coming in the kitchen. Billy, Mikey with the cat on a string, Julia and Vaclav the Pole. It was fine, they had nowhere to go. But this one night, Mikey's cat, sort of, did a, a, a sort of a shit, on a chopping board. And Hal and Allie get a bit upset and there were words and then Allie storms out and Hal follows and I go after them. I overhear them talking and Hal says, 'Why don't we ask Danny to talk to them?' And Allie says, 'Why would they listen to Danny more than us?'

He drinks.

'He's a rough-sleeper,' Hal says.

He smiles through the hurt.

It was fine. I knew what he meant. You know, they were all my mates, I've known them for years, and if they were going to listen to anyone it would be me. You know. Fair enough. I'd get through not because I'm a rough-sleeper, but because I'm fucking, I fucking know how to talk to them, and I know how to talk to the GA. I'm fucking – I can do it all. So I go back in and I round everyone up. 'Come on you lot, fuck off, this isn't a fucking zoo, piss off, we've got work to do.' And they all sort of fuck off one by one. And Hal comes up to me and says, 'Nice one, Danny, that was getting out of hand.'

He hides how pissed off he was.

(*Forced.*) And I'm glad.

Beat.

I am. 'Cause now I can see how stressed everyone was, and everyone starts talking to each other again, and it's like it's all back to normal with Wooky doing impressions and Allie slapping people with leeks and it's fun. Back to normal.

Beat.

Back to normal.

Beat.

Allie and Dev cooking, Hal and Wooky serving, me on washing up, everything back to normal. So I have no fucking idea why, when no one's looking, I go to the donation tin and nick twenty quid.

Beat.

Never stolen anything in my life. After losing my job, losing the dole, and the fights over money, had more fights over money than fucking – (anything), I never stole, ever. She fucking knows. Fucking standards. All you've got when you've got nothing. Fucking brought up right. Fucking bringing up a – (boy, right). You don't fucking steal. Whatever I got wrong, I taught him that. Fucking proud people. Just because I'm a rough-sleeper don't mean I haven't got any fucking pride.

He is confused.

I wanted to do some good with it. Yeah, I broke the Occupy rules, but I was doing something good with it. I bought some vodka, and found Mikey and Vaclav and shared it with them. Doesn't matter if it's a bowl of soup or a bottle of vodka, or some warmth from a fire, it's all fucking sharing. It's all about connecting people. I'd kicked them out of the kitchen, I don't want them thinking I'm taking sides. I'm not having any of that shit, I'm here to make sure no one slips out of the big picture. So we have a bit of party, few drinks, smoke, fire going, couple of jellies. Someone gets some music going, vodka goes round. We don't need the fucking tea tent, we can have a party on the camp.

'Why don't you lot fuck off somewhere else? It's four a.m.' And there's this bloke, in his sleeping bag, trying to put out the bonfire, shouting and swearing, and literally hopping mad, fucking jumping around on the fire. And then I see. 'Fuck me.'

Pause.

'It's Hal the Buddhist.'

Pause.

It's Hal the Buddhist. In his pyjamas, hopping up and down in a sleeping bag, trying to put our fire out.

'Don't do that, Hal. Don't do that we're freezing.'

But he carries on.

'Hal, please.'

'I don't give a shit, there's fucking tents everywhere, you could kill someone, you stupid fucking pisshead.'

And I grab him.

He catches his breath.

I just grabbed him. But next time I go to the kitchen it's pissing it down, and Carol's waiting for me.

Beat.

It's weird because she's standing inside, and then when she sees me she steps outside. So we both stand there, in the rain.

'They told me to tell you, you can't come in. You're not welcome.'

'Why?'

'Because . . . '

He is ashamed.

'Because you knocked one of Hal's teeth out.'

It pains him to remember this.

I try to get past her, but each time she steps in my fucking way, like it's a fucking dance, and I fucking . . . 'OUT OF THE WAY, PONCHO', and Allie hears and steps out into the rain. And it's just me and her. And when I see her, getting soaked, to be with me, I want to say, I want to say I'm sorry. I want to say thank you. I want to say, even though I've got a hole in my life, somehow, you make it OK. I want to say, some days just standing next to you is enough.

Beat.

I've got all this stuff I want to say, and I know if I can just tell her, all this will be sorted out. But I don't say any of that. I say:

'He fucking deserved it.'

He is devastated.

Beat.

I didn't want to fight with her. I didn't want to fight with any of them. I don't know why everything I did upset everyone. I didn't want to take sides, but everyone else was. Everyone was fighting. You couldn't go two yards without getting into a fucking argument. They couldn't fucking see that I can't lose any more people in my life. Everything they were fighting about was bollocks. In the big picture it was bollocks. They got their own police force. Tranquillity. That pissed everyone off, but I didn't mind, I just wanted everyone to stay together. Everyone gets upset that they close the tea tent, but Tranquillity get a new tent with sofas and burners and DVD players. I don't give a shit, it's not important, give them a fucking swimming pool if it stops the arguing.

Beat.

I make myself eat in the kitchen. I keep my head down, don't cause any trouble. They might not want me, they might ignore me, but I'm still eating with them. I don't care, I'm not embarrassed. I'm not going back to the soup kitchens. I'll eat there even if no one talks to me, because I'm not giving up. For the first time in the whole fucking Occupation, I'm glad Carol's there because she's the only one who speaks to me. She's actually quite a nice old lady. Poncho. She's a grandmother. She chats to me and everyone else carries on. I'm in there, and Carol serves me, and we have our chat that we always have about how cold it is, and then she says:

'Danny, love, you can't bring that in here.'

Beat.

I don't know what she's talking about for ages but then I realise she's pointing at my can.

'The camp's a drug- and alcohol-free zone.'

Pause.

'Since when?'

'Since the GA decided.'

Beat.

Which is fine.

Beat.

But then I see the rest of them, all of them, Dev, Allie, Hal, Wooky, and they've all gone quiet. No one's talking. Because they all want to see what I'll do. See what the alki'll do.

Beat.

So I pour it away.

He pours it over his head.

And they ban me from the kitchen.

He is reborn as his former self.

They want an alki, I'll be a fucking alki – seven years I've been drinking on those steps and they want to try and fucking tell me what to do? Fuck off. Banning me from places, telling me to move on, they've got a police force chasing me around, what's the difference between Occupy and the City of London? How can you change the world, when you can't fucking keep a kitchen open to people? I see it, I see it all, I see it before any of those cunts. And I won't fucking stand for it. So I get prepared, I get prepared. I know what they're gonna do next, they're all planning legacy and what to do after the eviction. So when the result comes in, I've got no fucking choice. I'm the only one who fucking cares any more. I fucking tie the doors down. I pull the shelves off and build a barricade and fucking occupy the kitchen myself.

'YOU'RE NOT COMING IN. I FUCKING KNOW WHAT YOU'RE GONNA DO.'

He picks up an imaginary frying pan.

'I DON'T GIVE A SHIT IF WE LOST A COURT CASE. TOUCH THIS KITCHEN AND I'LL STAB YOU.'

'WHAT THE FUCK HAS HAPPENED TO YOU? MAKING PEOPLE HOMELESS, BANNING DRINKING. GOT YOUR OWN POLICE. YOU'RE NO BETTER THAN THE CITY. The only thing we've got is this kitchen and you're not taking that away from me.'

Beat.

'WHO ARE YOU? NONE OF YOU USE YOUR REAL NAMES.'

Beat.

'YOU CAN'T FUCKING COME HERE. AND GIVE ME ALL THIS AND THEN TAKE IT AWAY.'

'I WILL NOT GO BACK TO THE STREET. I'VE GOT GAS IN HERE, I'LL SEND THE WHOLE FUCKING PLACE UP. YOU CAN'T MAKE ME. YOU CAN'T. I DON'T GIVE A FUCK WHAT ANYONE SAYS. NOT THE JUDGE, NOT THE JUDGE, NOT FUCKING TRANQUILLITY. I AM NOT GOING BACK. I AM NOT GOING BACK TO THE STREETS. I CAN'T GO BACK. I CAN'T BE ON MY OWN. I can't. I can't. I can't. I can't. I can't.'

He drops to his knees and tries to pack his bag.

I can't, I can't I can't I can't I can't I can't.

He starts to look for his phone.

I can't I can't I can't I can't I can't, where's my phone?

Crying, he goes through his bag, he finds his phone, but he also finds an Anonymous mask.

He pulls it out and holds it at arm's length. He considers it, for what feels like an age, as he remembers his son, and Occupy.

Pause.

You know. I could bear it. I could bear it all. I could. I had it all figured out. How to bear living with myself. With what I've done. I could bear it. And then you lot come along. And now look at me.

He grabs the phone and throws it against the set.

He smashes the set up.

Five

LOOK AT ME.

At patrons.

DON'T FUCKING LOOK AWAY. LOOK AT ME.

At patrons.

WHAT DO YOU SEE?

At patrons.

WHAT AM I MISSING?

At patrons.

A FLAT?

Beat.

A BEDSIT IN FULHAM?

Beat.

THAT GONNA MAKE EVERYTHING OK, IS IT?

Beat.

DOES IT MAKE YOU HAPPY?

Beat.

WITH YOUR PHONES.

Beat.

AND YOUR MORTGAGES. ARE YOU HAPPY?

Beat.

ARE YOU SAFE?

Beat.

YOU WISH THAT FOR ME?

Beat.

A BEDSIT?

Beat.

I DON'T WANT IT. I don't need reminding my life is
ruined. You think I don't know that? You think I don't know
everything worth living for is gone. For ever.

Beat.

I don't need reminding of that. I need, I need reminding I have
something to offer.

Beat.

I have something I can do. I can make something better. I can
make someone's life better. Even if it's just a bowl of soup.

Beat.

I can do that.

Beat.

I know I can. I might be able to help you with something.

Beat.

Just need the chance.

Pause.

I don't want a bedsit, I want someone to talk to. If I wake up
frightened I want someone there. If I'm sad I want someone
to cheer me up. If I feel useless I want a job. If I feel stupid
I want to learn. And I'll only ever get that from you.

Silence.

Occupy screwed my life up.

Beat.

Because it gave me hope.

He discards the mask.

The mobile starts to ring, but he doesn't answer.

He turns his back to the audience and starts to walk out.

We are left with three points of focus. The mobile phone, the rough-sleeping gear, the Anonymous mask.

Danny *walks offstage.*

Lights down.

DRAMA ONLINE

A new way to study drama

From curriculum classics
to contemporary writing
Accompanied by
theory and practice

Discover. Read.
Study. Perform.

Find out more:
www.dramaonlinelibrary.com

 FOLLOW US ON TWITTER @DRAMAONLINELIB

 BLOOMSBURY

 methuen drama

 AS THE ARDEN SHAKESPEARE

 ff FABER DIGITAL

Bloomsbury Methuen Drama Modern Plays
include work by

Bola Agbaje	Robert Holman
Edward Albee	Caroline Horton
Davey Anderson	Terry Johnson
Jean Anouilh	Sarah Kane
John Arden	Barrie Keeffe
Peter Barnes	Doug Lucie
Sebastian Barry	Anders Lustgarten
Alistair Beaton	David Mamet
Brendan Behan	Patrick Marber
Edward Bond	Martin McDonagh
William Boyd	Arthur Miller
Bertolt Brecht	D. C. Moore
Howard Brenton	Tom Murphy
Amelia Bullmore	Phyllis Nagy
Anthony Burgess	Anthony Neilson
Leo Butler	Peter Nichols
Jim Cartwright	Joe Orton
Lolita Chakrabarti	Joe Penhall
Caryl Churchill	Luigi Pirandello
Lucinda Coxon	Stephen Poliakoff
Curious Directive	Lucy Prebble
Nick Darke	Peter Quilter
Shelagh Delaney	Mark Ravenhill
Ishy Din	Philip Ridley
Claire Dowie	Willy Russell
David Edgar	Jean-Paul Sartre
David Eldridge	Sam Shepard
Dario Fo	Martin Sherman
Michael Frayn	Wole Soyinka
John Godber	Simon Stephens
Paul Godfrey	Peter Straughan
James Graham	Kate Tempest
David Greig	Theatre Workshop
John Guare	Judy Upton
Mark Haddon	Timberlake Wertenbaker
Peter Handke	Roy Williams
David Harrower	Snoo Wilson
Jonathan Harvey	Frances Ya-Chu Cowhig
Iain Heggie	Benjamin Zephaniah

Bloomsbury Methuen Drama Student Editions

Jean Anouilh *Antigone* • John Arden *Serjeant Musgrave's Dance* •
Alan Ayckbourn *Confusions* • Aphra Behn *The Rover* • Edward
Bond *Lear* • *Saved* • Bertolt Brecht *The Caucasian Chalk Circle* •
Fear and Misery in the Third Reich • *The Good Person of Szechwan* •
Life of Galileo • *Mother Courage and Her Children* • *The Resistible
Rise of Arturo Ui* • *The Threepenny Opera* • Anton Chekhov *The
Cherry Orchard* • *The Seagull* • *Three Sisters* • *Uncle Vanya* • Caryl
Churchill *Serious Money* • *Top Girls* • Shelagh Delaney *A Taste of
Honey* • Euripides *Elektra* • *Medea* • Dario Fo *Accidental Death
of an Anarchist* • Michael Frayn *Copenhagen* • John Galsworthy
Strife • Nikolai Gogol *The Government Inspector* • Carlo Goldoni
A Servant to Two Masters • Lorraine Hansberry *A Raisin in the
Sun* • Robert Holman *Across Oka* • Henrik Ibsen *A Doll's House*
• *Ghosts* • *Hedda Gabler* • Sarah Kane *4.48 Psychosis* • *Blasted* •
Charlotte Keatley *My Mother Said I Never Should* • Bernard Kops
Dreams of Anne Frank • Federico García Lorca *Blood Wedding*
• *Doña Rosita the Spinster* (bilingual edition) • *The House of
Bernarda Alba* (bilingual edition) • *Yerma* (bilingual edition) •
David Mamet *Glengarry Glen Ross* • *Oleanna* • Patrick Marber
Closer • John Marston *The Malcontent* • Martin McDonagh *The
Lieutenant of Inishmore* • *The Lonesome West* • *The Beauty Queen
of Leenane* • Arthur Miller *All My Sons* • *The Crucible* • *A View
from the Bridge* • *Death of a Salesman* • *The Price* • *After the Fall* •
The Last Yankee • *A Memory of Two Mondays* • *Broken Glass* • Joe
Orton *Loot* • Joe Penhall *Blue/Orange* • Luigi Pirandello *Six
Characters in Search of an Author* • Lucy Prebble *Enron* • Mark
Ravenhill *Shopping and F***ing* • Willy Russell *Blood Brothers* •
Educating Rita • Sophocles *Antigone* • *Oedipus the King* • Wole
Soyinka *Death and the King's Horseman* • Shelagh Stephenson
The Memory of Water • August Strindberg *Miss Julie* • J. M.
Synge *The Playboy of the Western World* • Theatre Workshop
Oh What a Lovely War • Frank Wedekind *Spring Awakening* •
Timberlake Wertenbaker *Our Country's Good* • Arnold Wesker
The Merchant • Oscar Wilde *The Importance of Being Earnest*
• Tennessee Williams *A Streetcar Named Desire* • *The Glass
Menagerie* • *Cat on a Hot Tin Roof* • *Sweet Bird of Youth*

Bloomsbury Methuen Drama World Classics
include

Jean Anouilh (two volumes)
John Arden (two volumes)
Brendan Behan
Aphra Behn
Bertolt Brecht (eight volumes)
Georg Büchner
Mikhail Bulgakov
Pedro Calderón
Karel Čapek
Peter Nichols (two volumes)
Anton Chekhov
Noël Coward (eight volumes)
Georges Feydeau (two volumes)
Eduardo De Filippo
Max Frisch (two volumes)
John Galsworthy
Nikolai Gogol (two volumes)
Maxim Gorky (two volumes)
Harley Granville Barker
(two volumes)
Victor Hugo
Henrik Ibsen (six volumes)

Alfred Jarry
Federico García Lorca
(three volumes)
Pierre Marivaux
Mustapha Matura
David Mercer
(two volumes)
Arthur Miller (six volumes)
Molière
Pierre de Musset
Joe Orton
A. W. Pinero
Luigi Pirandello
Terence Rattigan
W. Somerset Maugham
August Strindberg
(three volumes)
J. M. Synge
Ramón del Valle-Inclán
Frank Wedekind
Oscar Wilde
Tennessee Williams

Bloomsbury Methuen Drama
Classical Greek Dramatists

For a complete listing of Bloomsbury
Methuen Drama titles, visit:

www.bloomsbury.com/drama

Follow us on Twitter and keep up to date
with our news and publications

@MethuenDrama

Printed in Great Britain
by Amazon

52014537R00037